D0577979

HELLO AUTUMN!

SHELLEY ROTNER

Holiday House • New York

Summer is ending.

Autumn is coming.

The last flowers
bloom.

Sunflowers **hang**
their heavy heads.

Insects **sing** their
good-bye song.

Swallows **swoop**.

Change is in the air.
It feels **cool** and
crisp.

The days get **shorter**.
The shadows get **longer**.

Trees and plants spread their **seeds**.

New ones can **grow** in the spring.

Milkweed seeds **dance** in the wind.

Acorns and pinecones **scatter** on the forest floor. Maple seeds **twirl** to the ground.

Autumn is here!

Yellow, gold, red, and orange leaves . . .

fly and fall

to the ground.

We gather bouquets of beautiful **leaves**
and rake and jump in **colorful** piles.

Cold temperatures at night bring morning **frost**.

Animals **get ready** for the cold days ahead.

Squirrels collect and **store** nuts and build cozy nests.

Owls **find shelter** in hollows in trees.

Sheep and horses grow thicker **coats** to stay warm.
Dogs and cats do too.
Birds grow more **feathers**.

Soon, turtles will bury themselves deep in mud.
Snakes and earthworms will burrow underground.

Some animals **migrate:** they go south to find food, to stay warm, or to breed.

Other animals get ready to go into a **deep** sleep until spring. Bees **store** extra honey in their hives.

Bats and bears find **caves**.

Some frogs will **sleep** in muddy ponds.

People are getting ready for winter too.

We **harvest** the last crops—carrots, pumpkins, squash, and apples.

Cranberries float and turn **red**.
Cornstalks turn **golden**.

Many people **preserve** food to eat through the winter. We put our gardens **to bed** with covers of leaves.

Autumn is the time to celebrate Halloween!

And Thanksgiving!

We give thanks for the bounty of food from our earth.

The trees have lost their leaves and are **bare**.

The soil is **cold**, the ground is hard.

The days are getting **shorter** and shorter.

And then, it's the **shortest** day of the year, and winter is here!

Autumn Facts

Dedicated to Charlie girl.

Special thanks to Dr. Linda Henderson
and designer Katie Craig.

Copyright © 2017 by Shelley Rotner
All Rights Reserved
HOLIDAY HOUSE is registered in the U.S. Patent
and Trademark Office.
Printed and bound in April 2017 at Hong Kong
Graphics and Printing Ltd., China.
www.holidayhouse.com
First Edition
10 9 8 7 6 5 4 3 2 1
Library of Congress Cataloging-in-Publication Data
Names: Rotner, Shelley, author, photographer.
Title: Hello Autumn! / Shelley Rotner.
Description: First edition. | New York :
Holiday House, [2017] | Audience: 004-007.
Audience: K to Grade 3. | Identifiers: LCCN
2016058442 ISBN 9780823438693 (hardcover)
Subjects: LCSH: Autumn—Juvenile literature.
Classification: LCC QB637.7 .R68 2017
DDC 508.2— dc23 LC record available at
https://lccn.loc.gov/2016058442

Fall begins on the autumnal equinox, on or close to September 21. On this day there are about the same number of hours of daylight and darkness.

Throughout fall the days get shorter, and the nights grow longer. The sun is lower in the sky, and the air is cooler. The leaves on many trees turn colors and fall.

Why do leaves turn colors? Changes occur inside leaves. The job of a leaf is to make food. Leaves do this all summer long with the help of sunlight, water, carbon dioxide, and chlorophyll. Chlorophyll is what makes leaves green.

In fall there is less sunlight, and leaves can no longer produce food. They also produce a waterproof coating. With no water, leaves stop making chlorophyll. As the green chlorophyll goes away, other colors are visible, such as yellow, orange, and red. All fall leaves live on food that was stored during the summer. When all the stored food is used up, the leaf dies, turns brown, and falls.

Fall comes to an end on the winter solstice, which occurs around December 21. The winter solstice is the shortest day of the year and marks the beginning of winter.